The Beginners Guide to Meditation

How and why you should start meditating for a better quality of life!

Table Of Contents

Introduction iv

Chapter 1: Why Meditate? 1

Chapter 2: The Basics 5

Chapter 3: Focusing Meditations 8

Chapter 4: Watchfulness Meditations 14

Chapter 5: Guided Meditations 18

Chapter 6: Exploratory Meditations 21

Chapter 7: Constructing Your Own Ritual 22

Chapter 8: Continuing Your Meditation Education 23

Conclusion 25

Introduction

I want to thank you and congratulate you for downloading the book, *"The Beginners Guide to Meditation"*.

This book contains helpful information on the benefits of meditation and how you can start practicing it!

Meditation has existed in cultures around the world for eons, and has lasted up until present time for one reason – it works. Meditation has a range of benefits, both to the body and mind. As outlined in this book, it's easy to begin practicing, and it won't take long for you to notice a change in yourself as a result.

This book will explain to you techniques and tips for successfully meditating for a better quality of life. So hesitate no longer, and with the help of this book, begin experimenting with the age-old phenomenon known as meditation!

Thanks again for downloading this book. I truly hope you enjoy it!

Chapter 1: Why Meditate?

Meditation – doctors prescribe it, successful individuals recommend it, and people you know talk about it approvingly. Although meditation seems to be a modern fad, it is really a very ancient practice stemming from diverse parts of the world such as India, Europe, Japan, China, and many other lands. Meditation stuck until this day not only because there's a lot of culture attached to it, but also because a person who meditates experiences significant benefits in many areas of their life:

A Healthier Body

There are medical studies that have discovered the good effects of meditation on a person's body, namely:

- Lowering of high blood pressure
- A boost of energy
- Improved immune system functioning
- Decrease in the frequency and severity of asthma, cancer, and other chronic illnesses
- Less fatigue
- Greater control over pain

- More relaxed sleep
- Better posture
- Stronger will to avoid indulgence in harmful substances or behaviors
- Motivation to pursue health-enhancing practices

When you meditate, you gain better control over your thoughts and feelings – two things that cause stress and stress-induced ailments if left unchecked. Meditating induces deep relaxation and this counteracts the negative effects of the stress hormone cortisol, which damages the body's cells and organs. It makes the body more efficient in managing itself, thus you get stronger resistance against diseases and you recover faster. You will also get more aware of your body and pay attention to what affects it – thus you catch yourself when you do something that's harmful to your health. Most importantly, a positive state of mind generates a craving for a healthier lifestyle, thus the simple act of meditating can lead to a major enhancement of life.

A Better Mind

A person's mind is likewise affected by meditation. These effects are not limited to a person's thoughts but also reach to the emotions and the hidden elements of a person's psyche. Meditation improves a person's mentality through the following methods:

- Gives ability to choose thoughts
- Brings back focus
- Eliminates distractions
- Improves emotional control
- Enhances clarity of perception
- Brings new perspective on things
- Improves ability to cope with stress
- Increases self-knowledge
- Boosts self-control
- Nourishes creativity
- Improves memory

As you will learn shortly, meditating allows you to let go of certain thoughts that you don't want to have. It gives you the opportunity to watch what goes on in your head and decide what to keep in there. You will see how your mind affects you so you can choose to think differently. You can change your thoughts so you can influence what you feel about things, and you can also make yourself think and feel whatever you want. You greatly improve your ability to concentrate and you will have a stronger memory. But even more interestingly, you will access parts of your mind that were usually unavailable to you. As a result, you will tap into a reservoir of insight and creativity like what geniuses do.

Chapter 2: The Basics

There are plenty of meditative techniques out there. You may try as many as you could before settling on a ritual. However, the most important thing is to be consistent once you have decided on a method. This is because meditation often takes some time before it can create noticeable and lasting effects. Also, the mind is not used to being kept still; you need to train it to follow your directions and you only do this by repeated practice. With that being said, here are some basic facts about meditation you should keep in mind:

- Meditating is focusing. It is either concentrating on a particular stimulus or concentrating on not having anything to focus on. Your undivided attention is the most important thing here. When you meditate, expect that you will work on your ability to concentrate.

- Meditation is best done regularly. Set aside time for meditation and make this a daily habit if possible. Make sure that you won't be disturbed while you're meditating to have a quality experience. Observe your daily routines and locate spans of time when you can safely evade distractions and obligations. You can meditate for about 5 minutes at the beginning while gradually increasing it to 15 minutes or more. A month of meditating everyday will give you tangible results.

- There are many ways to meditate. This book will give you a broad view of meditation and how it is practiced. Some of the steps given may appeal to you while others may only make it harder for you to meditate. Try doing as much as you could initially so you could get a feel of how styles vary from each other. If something doesn't work for you, drop it and move on to something else.

- Meditation should be comfortable for you. Don't mistake being uncomfortable as a sign that you are meditating correctly. On the contrary, the best way to achieve a meditative state is when you are not hungry, you are well-rested, you are seated in a position that's not painful to you, and when you're in a stress-free environment.

- You need to relax when you meditate. You can't reach where you want to go in meditation if you keep on worrying about whether you're doing it correctly or if you're forcing yourself to have certain experiences. Just do the techniques and simply attune yourself to your meditative focus and goals.

- You can join meditation classes. If you prefer being guided by someone else, then by all means join a meditation class. Some meditation techniques such as yoga and other related practices are technical and they need the guidance of a skilled teacher. You also get to socialize with other meditators when you're in a class. Just make sure to know as much as you can about the class, the techniques, and the teacher. You will find more about this towards the end of the book.

- Pay attention to the results. Meditating correctly should bring you good effects. If it makes your health deteriorate, mess up your mind, or make you suffer at work or in relationships, you're not doing it right! It's recommended that you keep a journal and tally your experiences to check your progress. Be prepared to let go of a routine if necessary.

Chapter 3: Focusing Meditations

There are meditations that require you to focus on a particular thing, such as words, images, a concept, or a sensation.

Mantras

Mantras are meaningful words or sounds that are vocalized repeatedly to help bring you to a deeper state of mind, such as Om, Hare-Krishna, Om Mani Padme Hum, etc. Some of these mantras are prayers to deities, some signify a religious concept, while others don't have meanings in themselves but have certain effects to the mind when uttered. You can explore different religious beliefs to know more about these mantras; Hinduism and Buddhism have plenty of these. However, you don't have to adapt a particular faith in order for you to meditate. Simply enunciating the mantras with your utmost attention is enough for you to have a meditative focus.

Affirmations

Affirmations are a form of mental programming that is mentioned either mentally or out loud. They are statements of what you want to happen or become. It is said in New Age thought that what a person focuses on becomes his reality, so if he repeatedly affirms something, he will manifest it in his life. If you want to still your mind and experiment on your manifestation powers, here's how to formulate an affirmation:

1. Think about your desires.

2. Make a statement about your desire that is easy for you to remember and recite.

3. Write it in such a way that it is happening right now. For example, "I am full of love and happiness."

4. Do not put negative words in it. Say, "I choose to do actions that truly benefit me." Instead of, "I will not do things that will harm me." People who studied the mind discovered that when something is worded with the word not or no, the mind will still focus on the thing that is being negated. Consider this: "Do not think of pink fluffy clouds" causes you to think the very objects that you are instructed to avoid. Thus, refrain from bringing into your mind anything that you would rather leave out.

5. Make your affirmations vivid and real to you. Bring in as much detail as possible. See yourself doing it and experience it with all your senses.

6. Repeat it as often as you can.

Single word

A single word will suffice for meditation. Choose a word you would like to focus your mind upon. You can use the word as a fixed point for your attention, in the sense that you will only see or hear the word to the exclusion of all other thoughts. Or, you can use the word as a launching point for other thoughts to come in, but constantly centering on the word's essence.

- Word as focus: Repeat your chosen word in the mind repeatedly during the entire meditation period. When thoughts or sensations creep up, brush them aside and return to speaking the word.

- Word as a seed for other thoughts: Say the word to yourself, pondering on anything you want about it. If you chose the word "Success" for example, you can ask yourself, "What does success mean to me?" "How do I know I am truly successful?" "What do I feel when I exhibit success?" Seek to define the word and to expand your understanding of it. Even though it seems as if you are wandering about in thought, your attention is still narrowed down by the word itself.

Concept

You can take any concept or idea and use it as a magnet for your attention. Select something that does not make you confused or agitated – remember: you need to have a peaceful mind in meditation. The more you meditate on a concept, the more you will notice it in your life. This is because the thoughts we focus on filter what we perceive, and our perceptions affect what we think, feel, and do. In effect, we create our own realities by mulling over certain ideas about it.

Probing Questions

Questioning can lead your mind to focus intensely on the search for answers. Find a good question for pondering. Some good questions are the following:

"What does life mean to me?"

"What are the most important things to me?"

"How do I know the things that I know?"

"What is my current situation teaching me?"

This type of meditation is good for changing your perspective and coming up with solutions. Answer your questions, question your answers, and even question your questions. Probe and probe until you are satisfied with your statements.

Zen questioning

There are questions or koans that have no definite answers and they only provoke your mind to work harder. These are commonly paradoxes or other vague ideas. For example, "Am I what I think I am?" or, "Who is asking the question?" These are very difficult to answer straightforwardly and will generate other questions. This challenging method of meditation allows you to discover some parts of you that you were not familiar with. You may find out your priorities, intellectual tendencies, hidden memories, fantasies, fears, gifts, limitations, and other valuable information about yourself. This is akin to stretching your mind to its limit. Consider this as a form of brain exercise and a way to get to know yourself better.

Images

You can focus on any image or images if you prefer to look at things rather than speak or hear them. Here are some things you can use:

- Scenery
- Work of art
- Meditative mandala
- Simple object
- Candle flame
- A dot on the wall

Stare at this image during the entire meditation without thinking about it. This is challenging because the mind is used to analyzing and describing what it sees. Your eyesight will blur as the minutes go by – let this happen. You will notice that the longer you practice this, the easier it will become to focus on anything even when you're not meditating.

Breath focus

Many traditions teach about focusing on breathing to become enlightened. It is believed that the breath is a sacred thing and it is equivalent to our life force and connection with everything around us. You do breath meditations by focusing on your breathing. Pay special attention to your respirations and do not think about anything else other than your breath.

Some breathing meditation techniques:

- Count every inhalation as 1 and every exhalation as 2. Do this for as many times as you can.

- Inhale for four counts. Exhale for another 4. Repeat all throughout the meditation.

- Inhale and exhale rapidly for about a minute.

Take note: don't force yourself to breathe unnaturally if you can't tolerate it. Meditation shouldn't make you feel ill. Also, if you have a medical condition, get your doctor's approval first before trying any breathing exercises.

Chapter 4: Watchfulness Meditations

The mind is so used to churning up thoughts that it loses track of reality. By bringing it back to what is actually happening, you achieve a better state of mind that is more perceptive and less stressed out. Being mindful of your present state frees up your mind from clutter that's caused by an overactive imagination and a restless mind. During meditation ask yourself the following:

"What am I doing right now?"

"What do I perceive right now?"

"What do I feel, both physically and emotionally?"

"What am I thinking right now?

You don't need to sit still for this. You may do walking meditations or any other activity while bringing your awareness to the task. Try to be meditative for as long as it's safe for you to be meditating to improve the way your mind functions overall.

Do not attempt to meditate if you need to be vigilant such as when you're on the road, using power tools, taking care of a child, working with delicate instruments, and the like.

Note: the vigilance you use in everyday situations is not the same as that in meditation. A meditative focus attends to as few stimuli as possible while your ordinary awareness normally covers many inputs at the same time.

Concentrating on the Emotions

Our emotions are usually beyond our grasp; they just happen and we get swept away by them. Paying attention to our internal conditions without attaching ourselves to them gives us the power of detachment, which lessens the hold of emotions on us.

Whenever you feel an unwanted emotion, simply let it in your awareness without adding to it. Analyze it – where did it come from? What caused you to feel that way? Could you choose to feel differently? If you let go of it, would its absence bother you? Confront its existence and see how far you could go to change it into a more desirable emotion.

Concentrating on Thoughts

Likewise, you can remove yourself from your thoughts and change them for the better. If a thought comes up, treat it like a temporary matter. Do not hold on to it; just shrug it off and continue whatever you were doing. The more you focus on thoughts or feelings, the bigger they get. Use your focus in controlling whatever grows in your awareness.

Do this exercise to know what's inside your mind.

You need your imagination for this. Pretend that you are in a place where you can be at peace (example: in outer space, in your garden, or in a castle). Say to yourself that you want to see what's in your mind. Let thoughts come up in balloons, and then prick them away. If a thought comes up, imagine them to be enclosed in a balloon or a similar object and then make them disappear. When you are just beginning, you will have many of these balloons but they will gradually decrease as you get used to thinking less and less.

Focusing on your Body

There are meditations that involve movement. These require skill and coordination, which forces your mind to focus on what it is doing:

- Yoga
- Qi-gong
- Tai-Chi
- Martial arts

These practices assume the existence of an energy that circulates within and outside our body. The movements aim in facilitating the proper flow of this force and in bringing greater control over our bodies and minds.

Paying Attention to Sensations

The senses may also be used to guide the awareness. It may be a song, a type of food, a fragrant object, a textured cloth, or anything that you would like to focus your senses on. Fix your attention in sensing and experiencing the item. Refrain from making any internal dialogues about it; just let yourself feel what your sense organs perceive.

Paying Attention to Nothing

This may be the hardest of the meditations yet. During this meditation, you will force yourself to be a complete blank. You will not think or feel anything at all. Sensory deprivation, or blocking your senses through blindfolds, earmuffs, and similar methods also belong to this category. It is best if you let a skilled teacher guide you through the process because of its difficulty and inherent dangers.

Chapter 5: Guided Meditations

Guided meditations lead your mind into a meditative level. These make use of instructive storytelling.

Structure of Guided Meditations

1. Relaxation induction – physical and mental
2. Instruction to put your mind into a deeper level
3. Exploration of the altered state
4. Bringing back into normal awareness gradually
5. Ending of the meditation

Example

Are you ready to meditate? I want you to close your eyes and take deep breaths...inhale...exhale. Inhale...exhale... let every breath you take bring you to an increasingly more relaxed state of mind. Relax your muscles – if you prefer, clench and unclench them until you feel more comfortable. Relax your head...your face...your neck...your shoulders...your chest...your stomach...your back...your hips...your thighs...your legs...and feet. Feel the relaxation envelop your entire body.

Now that you are feeling perfectly comfortable, begin to relax your mind. Leave your worries behind and focus on meditating. Imagine a pleasant scene or anything that relaxes you: a view of the mountainside, lying on a white cloud, a rainbow on the horizon… anything that gives you a very profound feeling of calmness. Simply observe it and experience it in your mind, without talking about it to yourself.

Imagine a stairway leading down, or anything that will give you a sensation of going deeper. This is symbolic of your journey towards your deeper, stiller mind. Count from 10 to 1, with each count leading you to go deeper. Ten, nine, eight, seven, six, five, four, three, two, one. You are now in a deeply relaxed state.

Explore your surroundings. What do you see? What do you want to do while you're in this place? You can examine your thoughts and feelings here. If you have a problem you would like to solve, you can tackle it here and you will find it much easier to deal with. You can program yourself with anything you want, and you will listen to yourself more fully. This is your meditative level and you can do amazing things with it.

I'm now bringing you back to your normal awareness. Remember you can go back to this place anytime you want for as long as you know how to relax your body and mind. Find the staircase and prepare to climb back up. I will count from 1 to 10, each time bringing you up to your normal awareness. One, two, three, four, five, six, seven, eight, nine, ten. Open your eyes slowly. You are back.

Making your Own Guided Meditation

You will find a lot of ready-made guided meditations like the one above, but you can make your own if you prefer a more personal touch. It is better if you record your guided meditation so you can play it later on when your eyes are closed. You can also read the meditation but you may not be as relaxed as when you shut your eyes since a lot of stimuli enter our eyes, and as you recall, more stimuli = less relaxation.

Chapter 6: Exploratory Meditations

When in a meditative state, explore anything you want about your mind. You can solve problems here - ask yourself the question and patiently wait for anything to come up. You might hear the answer, or see a picture or a scenario in your mind that points out the solution.

You have access to a greater amount of your brainpower during meditation so take advantage of this condition. You might even have psychic and paranormal experiences while at this state.

Chapter 7: Constructing Your Own Ritual

You can mix and match the previous exercises according to your preferences and needs. For example, you may do qi-gong, do body relaxations, and then focus on the breaths last. Make sure you have enough time to practice your ritual, and you have to practice it regularly for it to be most effective.

Write down your ritual or make a guided meditation on audio. Modify your steps if you want and if you intend to experiment on results. Always remember: if you have found a satisfactory routine, stick with it and increase the length of your meditation to boost your brain muscles.

Chapter 8: Continuing Your Meditation Education

If you want to evolve in your meditative ability, continue your research by attending meditation classes and immersing yourself in the different meditation practices. Be disciplined in your practices and see whether you are improving or not. If you are, then keep it up, but if not, examine where you need to focus on and strive to be better. The mind is like a muscle – it has to be trained regularly for it to work stronger.

When you are learning more about meditation, here are some things to look out for:

- You should get well with the teacher. A meditation teacher must have a pleasant personality. Don't mistake attitude problems as something that is educational for you. Meditation doesn't have to be learned the hard way, and the teacher doesn't have to punish or tire you out so that you could meditate correctly.

- You can try various meditation techniques. Some schools of meditation prohibit their students from studying other practices – beware of these! You have the right to learn what's out there so you can decide what's best for you. Teachers who shield their students from other schools of thought may be intending to keep them within the group to exert full control over them. The best teachers will not curtail your freedom but help you meditate to the best of your abilities, whether you decide to be loyal to them or not.

Conclusion

Thank you again for downloading this book!

I hope this book was able to help you learn more about meditation and why there's so much hype about it!

The next step is to put these steps in to practice, and begin meditating for a better and more enjoyable life!

Finally, if you enjoyed this book, please take the time to share your thoughts and post a review on Amazon. It'd be greatly appreciated!

Thank you and good luck!

www.ingramcontent.com/pod-product-compliance
Lightning Source LLC
LaVergne TN
LVHW021748060526
838200LV00052B/3547